Dinamation's
Dinosaurs

Campbell Books

Apatosaurus (ah-PAT-uh-sawr-us)

Apatosaurus means 'deceptive lizard'. Height: 4.5m, length 23m, weight: 30,000kg.
Also called brontosaurus, this creature had a very small brain and ate twigs and leaves.

Apatosaurus

Apatosaurus had four elephant-like feet, a long tail, and a small horse-like head
at the end of a very long neck.

Parasaurolophus (par-ah-sawr-OL-uh-fus)

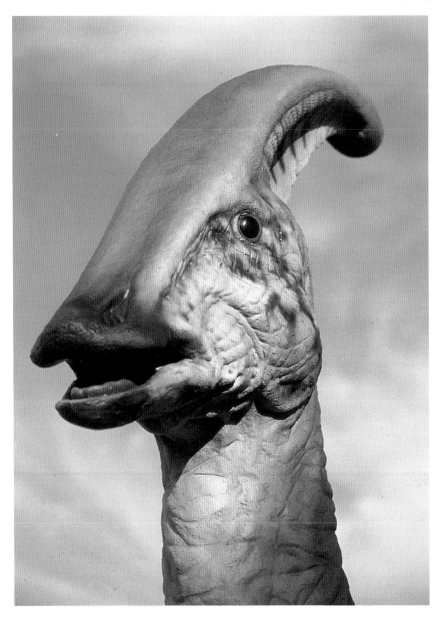

Parasaurolophus means 'similar crested lizard'. Height: 5m, length: 9m, weight: 3,000kg.
The head crest of this plant eating dinosaur was up to 1.8m long.

Stegosaurus (STEG-uh-sawr-us)

Stegosaurus means 'plated lizard'. Height: 3.3m, length: 7.6m, weight: 2,000kg.
It had a tiny brain, moved slowly, and swallowed vegetation without chewing.

Dimetrodon (dye-MET-ruh-don)

Dimetrodon means 'teeth of two sizes'. Height: 0.9-1.2m, length: 2.5m, weight: 70kg.
This carnivorous animal is not a true dinosaur, being very much older.

Tyrannosaurus (tye-RAN-uh-sawr-us)

Tyrannosaurus means 'tyrant lizard'. Height: 5m, length: 15m, weight: 6,500kg.
It is the largest known flesh eating animal ever to walk on earth.

Allosaurus (AL-uh-sawr-us)

Allosaurus means 'different lizard'. Height: 5m, length: 10.7m, weight: 4,000kg.
It fed on other dinosaurs, using its sharp claws to hold prey.

Allosaurus

Allosaurus had a powerful neck, strong wide-opening jaws and sharp pointed teeth.

Tyrannosaurus

When catching prey, tyrannosaurus used its sharp claws and huge jaws containing 15cm long teeth.

Triceratops (try-SAIR-uh-tops)

The horns of the young triceratops have not yet fully developed.
These dinosaurs ate plants, cutting them up with their horny beaks.

Triceratops

Triceratops means 'three horned face'. Height: 2.9m, length: 7.6m, weight: 5,000kg.
Triceratops used its horns and bony frill as protection against tyrannosaurus.

Dinosaur hatching

Dinosaurs laid small hard eggs like reptiles and birds do today.
This is how a parasaurolophus baby may have emerged from its egg.

Pachycephalosaurus (pak-ee-SEF-uh-lo-sawr-us)

Pteranodon (tair-AN-o-don)

Pachycephalosaurus means 'thick headed lizard'.
Height: 2.4m, length: 4.5m, weight: 2,000kg.

Pteranodon means 'winged' and toothless'.
Wingspan 7.6-9m, weight: 16kg. Fish eating.

Deinonychus (dyne-ON-ik-us)

Deinonychus means 'terrible claw'. Height: 1.8m, length: 3m, weight: 80kg. Carnivore.
The name for this dinosaur comes from the huge sharp claw on the hind feet.

Deinonychus

The swift and aggressive deinonychus may have hunted in packs.
Most of the killing was probably done by kicking with the hind feet.

Photographs © Dinamation International Corp.
The use of the photographs in this book
licensed by Dinamation International Corp.
© Campbell Books 1992
First published 1992 by
Campbell Books
3/4 Bartholomew Place · London EC1A 7HH

Printed in Hong Kong

ISBN 1 85292 158 7